Original title:
Sallow Glares Above the Griffin Chaff

Author: Sebastian Sarapuu
ISBN HARDBACK: 978-1-80562-481-3
ISBN PAPERBACK: 978-1-80564-002-8

The Celestial Dance of Dust and Dreams

In twilight glow, the stars align,
Whispers stir where shadows twine.
Each glint anew, a universe spun,
Embracing all, the moon's soft run.

Winds of change in quiet flight,
Carrying wishes into the night.
They twinkle high, like hopes untold,
In endless tales, their warmth enfold.

Fading Reflections of the Forgotten Skies

An echo lingers, soft and fleet,
Where once were dreams, now dusted feet.
Ghosts of laughter fill the air,
In memories lost, we find our share.

Clouds gather round, their secrets shared,
Whispered stories that none have bared.
Together they float, in silence weave,
A tapestry bright, yet hard to believe.

Chasing Fragments of Illumination

Through mottled streets of ancient stone,
We chase the light, yet feel alone.
Shadows elongate, stretch and bend,
In search of truths that never end.

Each flicker guides like a distant star,
Promising hope, though near and far.
Crackling sparks dance on the breeze,
Awakening dreams from slumbering freeze.

The Twilight Tapestry Unraveled

Threads of evening, softly spun,
Woven tales of day begun.
Breezes carry the stories told,
In colors bright, and shadows bold.

Yet with each pull, a layer fades,
Revealing secrets in the glades.
As night unfolds with velvet grace,
We seek the light in this hidden space.

Nightfall's Feathered Keepers

The owls call softly, night draws near,
In shadows deep, they loom and steer.
With eyes like lanterns, bright and wise,
They weave through branches, 'neath starry skies.

A rustle whispers, secrets unfurled,
In twilight's arms, a magic swirled.
Their wings, a tapestry of night,
Guardians of dreams, in silver light.

Each silent flight, a tale untold,
Of moonlit paths and whispers bold.
They soar with grace, yet seldom seen,
In dusky realms, their watch serene.

A feathered prayer, on zephyr's breath,
To weave the threads of life and death.
With every gaze, they pierce the gloom,
In night's embrace, where shadows bloom.

Glinting Remnants of Celestial Dance

Stars scatter like dreams on velvet skies,
Glinting remnants, where wonder lies.
The moon waltzes, in silvery grace,
Its glow illuminates the hidden place.

Comets blaze trails, in a silent sweep,
Carving night's canvas, where secrets keep.
In swirling colors, the cosmos sings,
Of timeless tales and enchanted rings.

Galaxies twirl in an endless spin,
While the world below hums soft within.
Each twinkle a wish, a heartfelt plea,
Linda in starlight, forever free.

Ancient songs drift from star to star,
Guiding lost souls, near and far.
In the whisper of night, let dreams take flight,
On glinting paths, through endless night.

Carnelian Sky and Mythic Beasts

As dusk descends, the sky ignites,
In shades of carnelian, wild delights.
With fiery hues and whispers bold,
Mythic beasts stir, their legends told.

Dragons soar through crimson clouds,
Cloaked in fire, fierce and proud.
Griffins dance on winds so fast,
In dreams of glory, shadows cast.

Across the horizon, a creature sounds,
A lyrical roar, where magic abounds.
A tapestry woven of myth and lore,
In the fiery dusk, forevermore.

With each sunset, new heroes rise,
In carnelian wings and knowing eyes.
Adventure calls, as fire meets sky,
With mythic beasts that fly so high.

Flickering Echoes in the Twilight

The twilight hums, a gentle song,
Where echoes linger, soft yet strong.
In fading light, the world takes pause,
Reflecting on wonders, with gentle cause.

Shadows dance, in whispers sweet,
As heartbeat drums, their rhythm meet.
Flickering candles, warm and bright,
Illuminate dreams in the quiet night.

The air is thick with tales anew,
Of heroes forged and spirits true.
In twilight's cradle, magic gleams,
In flickering echoes, we find our dreams.

So hold the night, embrace its tide,
With each soft echo, let love abide.
In the twilight's arms, we weave and spin,
Flickering joy, where all begins.

Whispers of the Celestial Heralds

Among the stars where secrets dwell,
The heralds sing their tales so fell.
With whispers soft like silken threads,
They weave the dreams that nightward spreads.

In twilight skies, the echoes bloom,
A cosmic dance dispelling gloom.
From ancient depths, their voices rise,
To paint the night with truth and lies.

Each shimmered light a story cast,
Of futures forged and shadows past.
They call to hearts that yearn to soar,
In galaxies where spirits roar.

Yet listen close, for secrets blend,
In twilight's arms, the whispers mend.
The celestial songs, both fierce and sweet,
Guide wandering souls on fate's own feet.

The Lure of Dusk's Embrace

In twilight's tender, soft caress,
The world awakes to quiet stress.
A cloak of shadows, deep and wide,
Lures the heart where secrets hide.

The horizon blushes deep and gold,
As daylight bows, the night unfolds.
Each whispered breeze, a lover's sigh,
The call of dusk, where dreams comply.

Beneath the stars, the spirits weave,
A tapestry that bids us leave.
To chase the night, to revel free,
In dusky arms, our souls agree.

Yet in this grasp, a hint of fear,
For shadows whisper things unclear.
But drawn we are, by dusk's sweet song,
In twilight's dance, we all belong.

In the Company of Ethereal Shadows

Beneath the moon's soft silver glow,
Ethereal shadows flit and flow.
With secrets draped in ghostly veils,
They whisper paths of ancient tales.

In every flicker, a story spurned,
Of love and loss, for which we yearned.
Through hallowed woods, they glide and roam,
Embracing the twilight like a home.

They beckon forth with spectral hands,
To join their dance in twilight lands.
The night holds magic laced with woe,
In haunted streets, soft echoes grow.

Yet fear not, for in shadows' grace,
You find the light of a hidden face.
In eerie whispers, your heart will find,
The solace sought and left behind.

The Grief of Forgotten Aviators

Above the clouds, where silence reigns,
The aviators bear their pains.
With wings of dreams, they soared so high,
Yet now their whispers fade and die.

In barren skies, their stories fade,
Left in the wake of choices made.
Each flight a promise, now lost in dust,
In realms of fate, fades hope and trust.

Beneath the stars, their voices weave,
For those who dared to dream and leave.
A nightingale of sorrow sings,
In memory of forgotten things.

Yet still they glide on spectral streams,
Their spirits soaring in our dreams.
Though time may cloak their tales in tears,
Their journeys echo through the years.

The Harbinger of Dusk's Descent

As shadows stretch their weary arms,
The sun bows low, its warmth withdraws.
Whispers weave through twilight charms,
A velvet cloak, the night applause.

Stars alight in frosted skies,
Their glimmer soft, a distant grace.
The moon, a guardian, gently spies,
On dreams that dance in shadowed space.

The trees, they murmur ancient tales,
Of secrets kept in bark and bone.
The evening breeze, how keenly sails,
Through silver leaves that hush and moan.

In this embrace of dusk's decree,
Lies magic spun like fine, soft thread.
A world awash in mystery,
Where every heart might dare to tread.

So let us bow to night in awe,
And cherish each deep, fleeting sigh.
For in the dark, where dreams can thaw,
The harbinger of hope draws nigh.

Beneath the Watchful Night

Beneath the watchful night's embrace,
The moonlight drips on petals fair.
Each creature stirs, in quiet grace,
Awake to wonders, none compare.

Soft crickets sing their lullabies,
While owls keep watch from branches high.
In starlit realms, where silence lies,
The world spins low, we breathe, we sigh.

A tapestry of dreams unfolds,
In silver beams and shadowed flights.
Each secret of the night, it holds,
The whispers shared by thieving lights.

The velvet hues, they softly blend,
As time drips slow, its gentle pace.
Through every moment, hearts descend,
To dance among the night's embrace.

So linger here, where magic sways,
Beneath the stars, in night's delight.
For in this dark, where silence lays,
We find our truth, our inner light.

Dreams Soar

On wings of twilight, dreams take flight,
they sail through clouds where shadows play.
With starlit eyes, they pierce the night,
Awakening wishes lost by day.

In whispered tones, the heart confides,
To galaxies where hopes reside.
As night unveils its velvet sides,
Our spirits dance, unbound, untied.

Each fleeting thought, a comet's gleam,
Flashes bright in the endless dark.
In dreams, we weave our brightest theme,
Though starlight fades, we leave our mark.

As dawn approaches, do not fear,
For every dream has found its place.
With every ending, whispers near,
Creating paths in time and space.

So let us walk where dreams abide,
And chase the phantoms of the night.
For in our hearts, they shall reside,
As echoes glow in dawn's soft light.

Sighs of the Wind-Blessed Creatures

In moonlit woods where spirits roam,
The wind whispers to those who listen.
Its sighs caress the earth as home,
And in each breath, the night does glisten.

The foxes dart in shadowed flight,
Their eyes aglow with mischief's spark.
While owls guard secrets, cloaked in night,
Beneath the cover of the dark.

Each rustle speaks of tales untold,
Of ancient paths and lost desires.
In nature's quilt, both brave and bold,
The quiet hints of past conspire.

The breezes hum a lullaby,
To lull the weary world to sleep.
With every sound, the nightbird flies,
Its serenade a promise deep.

So let us heed the whispers mild,
And tread with care through dusk's embrace.
For in the sighs, we are beguiled,
By the wind-blessed creatures' grace.

Flickers of Hope in a Dim Evening

When shadows rise and colors fade,
In dim-lit corners, whispers bloom.
A twinkling star, a promise made,
A spark remains within the gloom.

Each flicker dances, a fragile flame,
That lights the heart with gentle grace.
In evening's grasp, though none the same,
Hope intertwines through time and space.

Through trials faced and worn-out dreams,
The path ahead grows faint but bright.
For in the dark, where nothing seems,
A small spark shines to guide the fight.

So cling to those rare moments still,
Where kindness grows in darkest night.
For every shadow bends to will,
With flickers of hope drawing light.

Embrace the night with open hands,
And trust that tomorrow's dawn will rise.
In every heart, a chance still stands,
As hope ignites beneath the skies.

Beneath the Cloak of Enigmas

In shadows deep, where whispers dwell,
The secrets swirl, like a muted bell.
A dance of thoughts, both dark and light,
In cloaks of mist, they take their flight.

With every breath, they weave a tale,
Of hidden paths that rarely hail.
A tapestry of time and fate,
In every stitch, the hands of fate.

Beneath the stars, the dreams unfold,
In snippets rare, their truths are bold.
Yet in the quiet, doubt creeps near,
A gentle touch, a voice sincere.

Around the corner, laughter stirs,
A haunting sound that softly blurs.
Yet deeper still, the shadows glide,
And beg the heart to turn and bide.

But in that space, a spark ignites,
And carries forth through endless nights.
For every secret, there's a door,
Unlock the charm, and seek much more.

The Dreamscape of Vanished Realities

In twilight's haze, where dreams reside,
The echoes of the past collide.
A shimmering veil conceals the dawn,
In whispered tones, the night is drawn.

Faint visions swirl, like leaves in flight,
Dancing shadows in soft twilight.
Each flicker holds a story lost,
In the embrace of time's soft cost.

Yet beyond the veil, a flicker glows,
Of realms unseen, where mystery flows.
A tapestry of hopes and fears,
That bathe the soul in silent tears.

With every heartbeat, worlds collide,
The walls of sleep, our dreams abide.
In this realm, our thoughts entwine,
And lost realities gleam and shine.

Awake, we drift on thought's soft stream,
While slumber spins a tapestry dream.
For in the shadows, we shall find,
The echoes of a longing mind.

Fractured Stories Beneath the Pigeon Grey

In pigeon grey, the tales ascend,
Of fractured lives that twist and bend.
Each laughter hides a silent cry,
While timeless moments pass us by.

Beneath the clouds, the whispers grow,
In tangled webs, the sorrows flow.
With every glance, a memory fades,
In shadowed streets, where dreams cascade.

Lost stories linger in the mist,
Of love that vanished, peace dismissed.
Among the ruins, echoes reside,
In every crack, where hopes collide.

Yet still the heart, it seeks to mend,
A flicker bright around the bend.
For in the gloom, a glow shall spark,
And give us strength to brave the dark.

So let us tread with careful grace,
In fractured tales, we find our place.
For though the grey may cloak the view,
The stories breathe, forever new.

Tendrils of Night's Caress

In night's embrace, the shadows play,
With tender holds, they sway and sway.
Each whispered breeze, a secret's song,
Entwining hearts where they belong.

The moonlit glow, a gentle guide,
In this realm where dreams confide.
With tendrils soft, it wraps us tight,
And spins a web of pure delight.

Beneath the stars, the stories breathe,
In every thread, we weave and seethe.
Yet still, the night unveils its lore,
As shadows beckon to explore.

So take a step, embrace the dark,
With every flicker, there's a spark.
For in the depths of night we find,
A tapestry that's intertwined.

In every shadow, whispers lay,
A dance of dreams that softly sway.
So let us roam where magic dwells,
In tendrils deep, our story tells.

Murmurs of Ashen Horizons

Whispers of the past take flight,
Across the ashen skies so bright.
Memories linger, softly spun,
In twilight's grasp, the day is done.

Silent echoes blend with time,
A melody, a distant chime.
In shadows cast by hopes once clear,
The murmurs call, inviting near.

Winds of change, they sweep the ground,
Where dreams once danced, now silence found.
Yet in the heart, a spark resides,
A flicker where the truth abides.

Beneath the veil of dusky hues,
The brave are called, the lost shall choose.
To face the fire, to claim the night,
In ashes, find the path to light.

So let the horizon bleed anew,
With every dawn, a chance to view.
For from the dark, the phoenix sings,
In murmurings, a new life springs.

Chronicles in the Dust of Flight

Across the skies, the stories weave,
In dust of flight, we dare believe.
Each feathered tale, a whispered vow,
In every breeze, we feel it now.

The clouds, a canvas, vast and wide,
Embrace the dreams that will not hide.
High above, where echoes play,
The chronicles await the day.

Oh, wanderer, with heart so bold,
Seek out the legends yet untold.
In every gust, discover fate,
In moments caught, we contemplate.

With every passing star that glows,
The path of flight, it gently flows.
Awake the magic, chase the night,
In dust of dreams, find your delight.

So let your spirit soar and glide,
Through realms of wonder, take the ride.
In chronicles of skies so bright,
We write our lives in dust of flight.

Lamentations of the Wretched Air

In wretched air, the sorrows swell,
Where whispered tales of heartache dwell.
Each breath we take, a heavy sigh,
In echoes lost, the spirits cry.

And yet the winds contain a grace,
A solace found in empty space.
With every storm, a chance to breathe,
In chronicles, the hope we weave.

Among the clouds, the burdens weigh,
Yet light can pierce the darkest day.
For in the tempest's raging song,
We find the strength to carry on.

Lamenting for the dreams we chase,
In every gust, we seek our place.
With voices raised against despair,
We stand as one, in wretched air.

So take my hand; together rise,
Through wails of night, we'll touch the skies.
In lamentations, we shall find,
A tale of hope that's intertwined.

Driftwood Shadows in the Starlit Veil

Beneath the stars, the shadows blend,
As driftwood whispers tales to mend.
In twilight's grasp, the night unfolds,
With secrets wrapped in dreams of old.

The sea of stars embraces all,
As ancient echoes softly call.
In every driftwood, stories lie,
Of journeys guided by the sky.

With every wave, the tides will shift,
Unraveling the gifts we lift.
In starlit veils, our wishes swim,
In shadows deep, our hopes grow dim.

Yet still, we wander, hearts aglow,
Through mist and moonlight's gentle flow.
In driftwood shadows, truths remain,
A tapestry of joy and pain.

So let the night envelop us whole,
In its embrace, we find our soul.
For in the starlit veil, we see,
The magic of what's yet to be.

The Light That Once Was

In shadows deep where hope once grew,
A faint whisper lost to the morning dew.
Echoes of laughter, a shimmering trace,
Now held captive in time's tight embrace.

Flickers of memory dance in the mist,
Like fireflies trapped in twilight's tryst.
With every heartbeat, they long to break free,
Yet tethered they remain, a part of me.

Through valleys of time, I search for that spark,
In the heart of the night, where dreams leave their mark.
Though the light may wane, it never quite fades,
For the heart holds the means to mend what decays.

So I'll chase the echoes, with hands open wide,
To gather the fragments, no longer to hide.
For the light that once was will rise once again,
Illuminating paths through the shadows of pain.

Beneath the Winged Canopy of Night

Underneath the stars, where whispers convene,
The night wraps its arms in a blanket serene.
A hush falls around in a velvet embrace,
As dreams take their flight in this magical space.

Moonlight weaves silver through branches so fine,
Crafting tales of wonder, both yours and mine.
The secrets of ages are softly disclosed,
While shadows dance lightly, in twilight composed.

Beneath the wings of a night-riding owl,
The world spins unfettered, a cosmic howl.
Stars blink like lanterns in sweet, endless night,
Guiding the weary on till morning's first light.

In silence, we gather beneath darkened skies,
Where wishes take shape and the heart never lies.
Each star a reminder of paths yet unknown,
In the embrace of darkness, we're never alone.

A Tapestry of Lost Azure

In threads of azure, the stories are spun,
Whispers from oceans, secrets of sun.
Each hue a memory, a moment in time,
Woven together, our lives in their prime.

From sapphire waves to the cerulean sky,
Colors of moments, the reasons we sigh.
Every shade echoes the joy and the pain,
As we paint our journeys through loss and through gain.

The tapestry flickers with memories bright,
A canvas of laughter, a splash of delight.
Yet threads of the past often unravel and fray,
And azure dreams wander, both longing to stay.

In the fabric of time, we sew what we must,
Binding our hopes in the warmth of our trust.
With each gentle stitch, we reclaim what we've lost,
A tapestry woven, no matter the cost.

The Riddle of the Cloud-Crowned Skies

High above where the heavens breathe,
Clouds unfold secrets that nature bequeath.
In the dance of the gales, a riddle is spun,
Whispers of storms, and the promise of sun.

With every drift and swirl, a story is told,
Of thunderous passion and lightning's bold hold.
Yet in light's gentle caress, truth softly hides,
As daybreak reveals where the mystery bides.

Chasing the shadows, the dancers take flight,
In the canvas of dusk, from day into night.
The riddle unfolds as each moment draws nigh,
In the heart of the cloud-crowned, limitless sky.

So look to the heavens and ponder the view,
For magic lies waiting, concealed in the blue.
The riddle of life is a journey we share,
A testament woven in the cool evening air.

Whispers of Dusk Beneath Faded Wings

The evening sighs, soft as lace,
Where shadows pulse in a tender grace.
Faded wings brush the twilight air,
Whispers beckon, secrets to share.

In gardens where lost hopes reside,
Silvery glimmers of dreams abide.
Stars blink gently in their old flight,
Framing stories of the night.

With every murmur, the world slows down,
A realm unmade, of silence, a crown.
Time dances lightly, weaving its thread,
In the hush where but few dare tread.

Moonlight spills on the trembling leaves,
Carrying sighs of those who believe.
Beneath the soft blanket of dusk's embrace,
Faded wings carry us to a new place.

So linger now in this twilight dream,
Where nothing's quite as it may seem.
Let whispers guide you, gentle and true,
Beneath faded wings, find something new.

Shadows Dance in the Twilight Wastes

Shadows weave where the daylight wanes,
In twilight's grip, where silence reigns.
Ghostly figures twist and sway,
In the half-dark, they lose their way.

A flicker here, a murmur there,
Secrets linger in the cold night air.
Footsteps echo on the cobbled stones,
As if the ground remembers the bones.

Forgotten dreams take form and flight,
In the depths of this forgotten night.
Voices rise like mist from the ground,
In shadows, lost hopes can be found.

Time drips slowly in the gathering gloom,
Where echoes linger and nightflowers bloom.
What was once spoken in the light of day,
Hums softly now, as shadows play.

Embrace the dance of the whispered tales,
That twine through the night with their ghostly trails.
In twilight's embrace, all fears lose their hold,
As shadows dance, brave and bold.

Beneath the Scorn of Withered Skies

Beneath the scorn of the withered skies,
Where dreams once bloomed, now withered lies.
Hope, like dust, clings to the ground,
In the silence, a distant sound.

The sun has set on a fading plight,
Leaving echoes of an unfulfilled night.
Clouds gather thick, dark as regret,
Promises made, but none to be met.

In fields of gray, shadows drift and sigh,
As memories haunt the bones of the sky.
Life whispers soft through the brittle leaves,
Where heart's desires no longer breathe.

Twilight drapes in a veil of woe,
And yet within, a flicker glows.
Hold on tight to the threads of dreams,
For hope can thrive in the darkest seams.

So wander here with an open heart,
Beneath the scorn, where shadows part.
Let every whisper be a spark that ignites,
A tale reborn from forgotten nights.

Echoes of Worn Dreams Adrift

In the echoing halls of time's embrace,
Worn dreams flutter, seeking a place.
Adrift they sail on currents unseen,
Whispers of what might have been.

Each heartbeat tells a tale of the past,
Where moments shimmer, yet cannot last.
Hope like starlight flickers and fades,
In memories sweet, our laughter cascades.

The dawn peeks through a veil of mist,
Bringing forth a promise, a gentle twist.
Worn dreams rise to meet the light,
As shadows wane in the soft daylight.

Yet still the echoes linger on,
In twilight's song, they've not withdrawn.
Riding the waves of a fleeting sigh,
Dreams take flight, learning to fly.

So cherish the whispers that time allows,
For echoes of dreams are the heart's vows.
In the tapestry woven of old and new,
Find solace in what the night can construe.

Whispers of Dusk and Feathers

As dusk descends, the shadows play,
Feathers flutter, soft and gray.
A gentle breeze whispers tales untold,
Of secrets held in the twilight's fold.

The murmurs rise with the fading light,
Embodying dreams that take to flight.
In the quiet glen where fireflies gleam,
The world slumbers deep, lost in a dream.

Beneath the boughs where the owls reside,
Night creatures stir, their spirits wide.
With every whisper, a promise grows,
Of magic lurking where no one knows.

In the heart of darkness, hope ignites,
Lifting the veil on enchanted nights.
A symphony played by the wind's refrain,
Calls forth the stars, like diamonds in rain.

So linger a moment as shadows twine,
And let the whispers of dusk align.
For in this realm where the quiet reigns,
The feathers of night hold the world's remains.

Shadows Dance with the Winds of Uncertainty

Shadows gather, swirling and bright,
Dancing freely in the waning light.
Uncertainty weaves in every stride,
As the night beckons, a promise inside.

Through the forest, a gentle sway,
Wind carries whispers of night and day.
Branches creak in an age-old song,
Where time and space seem to belong.

Footsteps echo in the stillness here,
Where dreams collide with whispered fear.
Yet joy flickers like a candle's flame,
Drawing the lost back to the same.

With every gust, stories unfold,
Of brave hearts hidden and dreams retold.
In shadows where the soft moon beams,
The threads of fate unravel, it seems.

So join the shadows, let them lead,
For in their dance lies a daring creed.
In uncertainty's arms we find our way,
Where night turns bold, and dreams dare play.

The Echoes of Winged Watchers

High above, the winged watchers soar,
With silent grace, they ever explore.
Their cries echo through the sky so vast,
Guarding the secrets of the ages past.

With every flap, a story takes flight,
A tapestry woven of day and night.
Beneath their wings, the world is still,
In awe of beauty, a heart to fill.

They mark the passage of time's gentle hand,
Dancing through forests and over the sand.
In their shadows, old tales emerge,
Of valor, of sorrow, and of the urge.

From mountain peaks to valleys low,
The echoes of watchers continue to flow.
Each flutter and swoop, a tale to share,
Of those who wandered, seeking the rare.

So lift your gaze to the skies above,
Embrace the echoes, the pulse of love.
For in the flight of these winged kin,
Lie whispers of worlds yet to begin.

Twilight's Grasp on Forgotten Realms

In twilight's grasp, the past awakes,
A tapestry woven with heartache and stakes.
Forgotten realms emerge from the mist,
In the fading glow, they can't be dismissed.

Silhouettes dance at the edge of sight,
Where shadows are cast by the pallid light.
Memories linger like the scent of rain,
Calling forth dreams that still entertain.

Through ancient woods where the spirits roam,
The echoes of laughter create a home.
Each tree holds a story, a whisper, a sigh,
That sails through the air on the wind's gentle cry.

With every heartbeat, the night unfolds,
Embracing the dreams that twilight holds.
In this embrace, forgotten realms gleam,
Awakening hopes that flourish in dream.

So tread lightly on this sacred ground,
For in the twilight, the lost are found.
In the grasp of dusk, let your heart dwell,
In the magic of stories that time cannot quell.

A Dance of Lore Amidst Faded Remnants

In shadows deep where whispers dwell,
Old tales are spun, a magic swell.
Footsteps echo through mossy stone,
As stars above begin to drone.

A flicker of light from ancient roots,
Awakens quiet, forgotten fruits.
The air, it hums with secrets long,
Inviting all to join the throng.

Ghostly figures in moonlit glades,
Twirl in dance through forest shades.
Each twirl a story, each leap a sigh,
Binding the past, as days slip by.

The echoes call from the evening's breath,
A song of life, a dance with death.
In every turn, a legacy fleeting,
A haunting melody, softly beating.

So weave your dreams with threads of gold,
Join the dance that never grows old.
For in this lore, we find our place,
A tapestry spun in time and space.

Threads of Twilight in Tattered Skies

When dusk unfolds its violet lace,
And daylight bids a soft embrace,
The whispers weave through twilight's hand,
Each thread a dream, each stitch a strand.

Above the clouds, a story glows,
Of ancient tales that no one knows.
They linger still in the fading light,
Adorned with hope, adorned with fright.

The shadows play where starlight meets,
And secrets swirl in twilight's skits.
With every breath, the magic sways,
In threads of dusk, where mischief plays.

A tapestry spun with hues of night,
Shapes the path down lanes of flight.
The moon looks down on paths once lost,
Illuminating dreams, no matter the cost.

So wander forth with open heart,
Let threads of twilight be your art.
For in the shadows, new worlds ignite,
Unraveling magic in the deepening night.

Wands of Memory in the Forsaken Breeze

In autumn's grasp, the leaves confide,
Secrets swirled, where dreams abide.
Wands of memory trace the air,
In echoes soft, flickering fair.

Through fields of gold and whispers low,
An unseen path begins to show.
Each gesture drawn from heart to hand,
A spark ignites on forgotten land.

The breeze carries tales of yore,
In sighs and laughs that we explore.
Each gust a memory, sweet or stark,
A reminder bright, a fleeting spark.

Forgotten wishes dance in flight,
Through twilight's veil, they seek the light.
With every wave of waning day,
Time bends and bows, then drifts away.

So wield your wand with gentle care,
For in each flick lies wonder rare.
Embrace the whispers, let them flow,
In forsaken breezes, dreams still glow.

Tattered Dreams Under a Weary Moon

Underneath the silvered glow,
Where tattered dreams begin to flow,
The moonlight dips in soft embrace,
Welcoming shadows to find their place.

A sigh escapes from weary hearts,
As starlit paths weave tangled arts.
Each heartbeat echoes in the night,
A longing song, a transient plight.

Among the ruins of hopes once bright,
Whispers linger, avoiding light.
Yet in the depths of faded schemes,
Lie fragments still of vibrant dreams.

A tapestry frayed by time's cruel hand,
Holds stories waiting to be spanned.
With every thread that dares to fray,
A new dawn beckons, come what may.

So gather the remnants, one by one,
Of dreams once lost, now found, now spun.
For under the weary, watchful moon,
Awakens hope, we're never alone.

The Descent of Faded Legends

Once bright and bold, the legends fade,
Whispers of glory in shadows laid.
Echoes of heroes, lost in time,
Their stories linger, an unspoken rhyme.

In halls of stone where memories sleep,
Ancient tales in silence creep.
From twilight realms, their spirits rise,
To weave through dreams like starlit skies.

Forgotten heroes in twilight's glow,
Sown in the past, yet still we know.
Their courage lingers, a heart's embrace,
In every shadow, their phantom trace.

The world around them softly sighs,
Unveiling secrets with muted cries.
For legends never truly die,
They find a home where echoes lie.

Through pages worn, their voices hum,
In every tale, a heartbeat drum.
They guide the lost with whispered light,
Turning darkened hours to radiant night.

Flightless Phantoms in Silent Echoes

In the quiet night, phantoms soar,
With wings of dreams, they seek for more.
Silence drapes the world in hush,
As fleeting shadows gently rush.

Once they roamed the skies so wide,
Now they linger, where hopes reside.
Their laughter, a breeze on sorrow's cheek,
In the stillness, their spirits speak.

Oh, haunting souls, so close yet far,
Trapped in the light of a distant star.
Flightless whispers on the moonlit path,
Dance through the night, invoking their wrath.

In every heartbeat, a tale unfolds,
Of lives once lived, and stories told.
Yet now they wander, lost in dreams,
Sailing on shadows, as silence teems.

In echoes soft, their memory flows,
A woven tapestry that gently grows.
In the arms of twilight, they softly drift,
Flightless phantoms, a celestial gift.

Veils of Dust Over Forgotten Realms

Veils of dust whisper through the air,
Shrouded worlds, forgotten with care.
Timeless secrets in shadows hold,
Stories untold, in silence bold.

Once vibrant lands, now cloaked in gray,
Each grain of time a price to pay.
With every breath, ancient silks sigh,
As wandering souls begin to fly.

Through crumbled halls where echoes prance,
Dance of shadows in a haunting trance.
Unseen magic lingers, yet to be found,
In the dust's embrace, mysteries abound.

The moonlight bathes the ruins bright,
Awakening dreams in the still of night.
For all that's lost can still be seen,
In veils of dust, where legends glean.

So let us explore, where memories wade,
In forgotten realms, our marks are made.
For every whisper holds a spark,
In veils of dust, we ignite the dark.

Shades of Twilight Wrapped in Silence

Beneath the cloak of twilight's grace,
Shades of silence find their place.
In colors dim, the world exhales,
As day retreats and twilight sails.

Wrapped in hush, the shadows creep,
Carrying secrets the night will keep.
Every moment, a fleeting sigh,
As dreams awaken and gently fly.

The stars emerge, a twinkling choir,
Igniting hopes like stars on fire.
In the silence, whispers conspire,
To weave the threads of lost desire.

Oft we wander through twilight's veil,
Searching for stories upon the trail.
Each step resonates with echoes deep,
In shades of silence, our hearts will leap.

Embrace the twilight, let shadows blend,
Where silence wraps, and dreams ascend.
For in the stillness, we find our voice,
Shades of twilight, in silence, rejoice.

The Dimly Lit Path of the Enchanted

In the hush of twilight's call,
Where whispers dance on shadows tall,
A path unfolds, lined with light,
Leading dreams into the night.

With every step, the secrets swell,
Tales of magic, spun so well,
Through ivy's grasp and moon's embrace,
Enchanting every hidden space.

The trees confide in silvery sighs,
While flickering stars weave ancient ties,
Guiding souls with gentle grace,
To realms where time can find its place.

A lantern glows with whispered lore,
Of heartbeats felt on distant shores,
As faeries flit on zephyr's breath,
Where dreams are born, and fears find rest.

So wander forth, young hearts take flight,
In the dimly lit path of night,
Where every turn might lead to more,
In the enchanted forest's core.

Chasing Shadows in the Ethereal Realm

In the realm where shadows play,
Where dreams and stardust drift and sway,
A chase begins, both wild and free,
Through twilight doors, to eternity.

Silhouette dancers weave their thread,
With laughter bright and whispers bred,
In twilight hues, they twist and twine,
As fleeting moments softly shine.

With every heartbeat, time takes flight,
In the dance of dark and light,
Fleeting echoes, a sigh, a glance,
Chasing shadows in spectral dance.

Each twirl a clock, each step a dream,
In the glow of an otherworldly beam,
Where the past and future intertwine,
In this ethereal realm divine.

So let your spirit rise and soar,
In the chase, seek forevermore,
Bound by magic, freed by night,
In the shadows' luminous flight.

Guardians of the Forgotten Twilight

In the hushed embrace of twilight's veil,
Guardians stand where memories pale,
Silhouettes keen, with eyes aglow,
Whispering tales of long ago.

Through mazes of mist, in silence they tread,
Warding the dreams that time has shed,
In the quietude, their strength aligns,
Binding the past with future signs.

With every breath, the echoes rise,
Enchanting winds and starlit skies,
Holding fast what shadows forget,
Guardians rise with no regret.

Amidst the stars, their secrets flow,
In twilight's glow, their power grows,
Protecting threads of lives once spun,
They guard the dusk till day is won.

So heed their call, in soft repose,
For in their watch, true magic grows,
Embracing all with gentle might,
Guardians reign in the twilight.

Mists of Memory and Feathered Dreams

In the mists where memories drift,
Soft as whispers, gentle as a gift,
A tapestry rich, woven with care,
Of feathered dreams that linger there.

Echoes of laughter, shadows of light,
In the heart's embrace, both day and night,
Through clouds of thought, the past will gleam,
In the tender touch of a fragile dream.

Time's delicate thread leads the way,
Through the memories that softly sway,
Every moment a heartbeat's trace,
In the mists, we find our place.

With every flutter, the spirits rise,
In feathered dreams beneath the skies,
Dancing gently on time's sweet seam,
Embracing the power of every dream.

So let the mists twine round your heart,
For in those whispers, life's true art,
With feathered dreams, let spirits soar,
In the mists of memory, forevermore.

Beneath the Clouded Horizon

Soft whispers flutter through the night,
Stars blink shyly, cloaked in light,
Winds carry tales on feathered wings,
Beneath the shroud, the shadows sing.

The moon reveals a hidden path,
Where dreams and fears entwine in laugh,
Footsteps echo on the ancient stone,
A journey where the heart is known.

The lake reflects a fading glow,
Ripples dance, secrets flow,
In the stillness, the spirits sigh,
Beneath the cloud, where visions fly.

Mountains loom with timeless grace,
Guardians of this sacred space,
They watch as dusk steals away,
Turning night to break of day.

Yet hope ignites in every heart,
As dawn unveils a brand-new start,
For in the shadows, magic lies,
Beneath the clouded, endless skies.

Where Myth and Twilight Intertwine

In the twilight, where shadows merge,
Myths awaken, begin to surge,
Woven threads of tales long past,
Echoing softly, endless and vast.

Whispers of dragons stir the air,
A flicker of hope, a maiden's dare,
Through enchanted forests, they glide,
Where secrets of the ancients reside.

Moonlit clearings hold their breath,
Guarding stories entwined with death,
The fae dance lightly on silken grass,
As moments of magic quietly pass.

Time suspends in the lavender haze,
Old legends flicker in feeble blaze,
As night weaves dreams with gentle hands,
A tapestry rich with far-off lands.

When daybreak breaks the spell so sweet,
Reality calls with steady beat,
But the heart knows where dreams reside,
In twilight's embrace, side by side.

Dreams Woven in Gilded Silence

In gilded silence, dreams take flight,
Whispers weave in the soft twilight,
Threads of hope, spun with care,
In slumber's grasp, we find our lair.

The world recedes, a distant sigh,
As night unfolds its velvet sky,
In shimmering pools of silver light,
Our thoughts dance through the endless night.

Each heartbeat carries a wish anew,
A canvas vast, a painter's cue,
With colors bright, our visions bloom,
In the quiet, dispelling gloom.

When dawn awakens with gentle hands,
Shattering dreams like frail bandstands,
Yet in the heart, their power lingers,
A melody played by fate's own fingers.

Though daylight calls with fervent plea,
The echoes of night setting us free,
In gilded silence, we still reside,
Where dreams and reality gently collide.

The Lament of Celestial Beasts

High above where starlights wail,
Celestial beasts weave their tale,
Majestic forms in endless flight,
Guardians of the lost, the night.

With wings unfurled, they roam the skies,
A chorus of sorrow, passion, cries,
Each echo a story of worlds once seen,
Of battles fought and spaces between.

In twilight realms, their shadows trace,
Magic remnants of a timeless place,
Where once they roamed with pride untamed,
Now in silence, their whispers framed.

The moon, their kin, sheds silver tears,
Collecting echoes of ancient fears,
As stars blink softly in mourning light,
For the lost, the brave, in the endless night.

But still their spirits wander on,
In every dusk, with every dawn,
As long as skies above still gleam,
The celestial beasts live on in dream.

The Specter of Worn Feathers

In shadows cast by ancient trees,
A whisper stirs upon the breeze.
With feathers frayed from years gone by,
The specter dances, soft and shy.

It haunts the dreams of those who dare,
To seek the truth, to seek what's fair.
Its sadness weaves like silver thread,
In tales of loss, where hope has fled.

Yet through the gloom, a glint remains,
A promise held through all the pains.
For every feather lost to flight,
New wings will rise to greet the night.

Oh, gather close, ye kindred souls,
And listen close to what it tolls.
For in the depths of worn-out dreams,
Life's magic glows in muted beams.

The specter sighs, with secrets old,
Of love and loss, of tales retold.
So let your heart feel every beat,
In every end, the chance to meet.

Gloomy Eyes of Unfurling Night

In twilight's grasp, the shadows creep,
With gloomy eyes, the night does weep.
It cloaks the world in velvety sighs,
Where whispered dreams and silence lies.

The autumn breeze begins its song,
A lullaby where shadows throng.
And there amid the curling fog,
A hint of fear, a playful smog.

With every star that dares to blink,
The night reveals what makes us think.
Inverted worlds, a cosmic dance,
Where fate and chance entwine the glance.

Yet in this dark, a spark can gleam,
As hopes emerge like spring's first dream.
For every tear that night bestows,
A brighter dawn, it gently sows.

So fear not, dear, the darkened plight,
For in the gloom, there lies the light.
In gloomy eyes, the heart can find,
The gem of love, forever blind.

Wraiths of Burdened Flight

Upon the wings of whispered winds,
The wraiths of burdened flight begins.
Through moonlit nights, they seek a trace,
Of stories lost in time and space.

With every flap, a shadow sweeps,
Across the dreams the silence keeps.
In haunting calls, they echo strong,
With melodies of right and wrong.

In tangled woods, they weave their way,
Creating paths where few can stay.
A dance of echoes, dark and bright,
In wraiths' embrace, we find our plight.

But from their flight, a lesson gleans,
To rise again despite the screams.
For in the burden, strength evolves,
As night surrounds, our heart resolves.

So watch them glide, the wraiths in flight,
Through haunted dreams in endless night.
For when we learn to bear the weight,
We find our place in love and fate.

Flickering Hues of Forgotten Glories

In twilight's blush, the colors play,
Flickering hues, they dance and sway.
With every shade, a tale unspooled,
In ancient whispers, softly ruled.

Beneath the surface, memories peek,
Of glories past, of voices meek.
In golden rays, the shadows blend,
To show us where our hearts can mend.

The canvas calls to those who yearn,
For every loss, a chance to learn.
In flickering light, we seek the past,
To find the truths that always last.

So let us cherish every hue,
And paint the skies with hope anew.
For while the glories may be gone,
Their flickering spark still lingers on.

With open hearts, we watch and wait,
For in our souls, we shape our fate.
Flickering hues, a hopeful plea,
In every sunset, we are free.

Wings of Fate in a Dusk-Kissed World

In a dusk-kissed world, where shadows play,
Wings of fate flutter, guiding the stray.
Whispers of dreams float on the breeze,
Finding their way through ancient trees.

Stars wink above in the deepening blue,
As secrets awaken, both old and new.
The night holds promises, wrapped in delight,
Embracing the wanderers, lost from the light.

Each heart, a compass, each soul, a spark,
Drawing connections from light to dark.
The echoes of laughter dance on the air,
Binding together what's fragile and rare.

Through meadows of wonder, with spirits unbound,
In moments of magic, true treasures are found.
With wings of fate resting gently near,
Guiding all travelers, both far and near.

The dusk holds the answers, the twilight's embrace,
Inviting the lost to unfold their grace.
In a world where fate whispers soft and sweet,
A journey begins with each heartbeat.

Secrets Stirred by the Fading Light

As the daylight wanes, secrets start to breathe,
In the twilight glow, truths gently weave.
Hidden in shadows, the mysteries stir,
In the fading light, the spirits confer.

The hush of the evening calls forth the past,
Voices of ages echo at last.
Like flickering flames, they dance in the night,
Illuminating tales veiled from our sight.

Each rustle of leaves sways with a song,
Inviting the curious all to belong.
With fireflies glimmering under the stars,
Mapping the pathways of love and of scars.

In canopies deep, dreams stir and entwine,
Whispered confessions, both yours and mine.
The magic of night cloaks our secret forms,
Cradling desires, transforming norms.

Riddles unfurl beneath the moon's gaze,
Translating the silence in whimsical ways.
In shadows we stand, holding hands tight,
As the secrets are stirred by the fading light.

Requiem of Lost Legends

In valleys unknown, where the old tales lie,
A requiem whispers, soft as a sigh.
Echoes of heroes, both noble and brave,
Now rest in the silence, the silence they crave.

For in every heart beats a story untold,
Of dragons, and journeys, of treasures and gold.
The myths of the ancients, now drifting away,
Like footprints in sand, as the tides sway.

With the whisper of leaves, the past fades and bends,
Carrying echoes of journeys, of friends.
The shadows of giants still linger and loom,
Their legacies woven through twilight's bloom.

Yet every lost tale holds the power to ignite,
A flicker of hope, a beacon of light.
Within the vast silence, their spirits remain,
Guardians of stories, through joy and through pain.

In each heart, the legends find home,
Invoking our courage to rise and to roam.
Though time may erase them, their essence will stay,
In the requiem sung, at the close of the day.

Celestial Whispers in the Gloaming

In the gloaming's embrace, where twilight is spun,
Celestial whispers drift, one by one.
Stars hold the secrets of worlds long ago,
Shimmering softly, casting a glow.

The night sings of magic, of hope in the dark,
Inviting the dreamers to leave a bright mark.
With each flicker of light, a wish takes its flight,
Guided by whispers, through silence of night.

Amidst the branches, where shadows entwine,
Celestial echoes beckon and shine.
In the yarns of the cosmos, our stories unfold,
Embracing the starlight, brave and bold.

In every heart beats a yearning so bright,
For guidance and wisdom, a spark in the night.
Through layers of stardust, our dreams take to sea,
Anchored in whispers, forever to be.

So listen closely, to the call of the skies,
In the gloaming's sweet breath, the essence will rise.
With celestial whispers, we find our own way,
As we dance with the stars, in the night and the day.

Ethereal Sentinels of the Narrow Path

Under ancient boughs, shadows grow,
Guardians watch where few dare to go.
Whispers weave through leaves so thin,
A dance of secrets where none have been.

Glowing embers in twilight skies,
Echoes linger, like soft goodbyes.
The narrow path beckons the brave,
With each step taken, the heart will crave.

Misty figures, cloaked in light,
Guide the wanderer through the night.
In the silence, a truth will unfurl,
A promise hidden in the world.

Stars above, like eyes that see,
Chart the dreams of what could be.
Ethereal sentinels, wise and bright,
Holding secrets of wonder and flight.

As dawn approaches, shadows fade,
In this place where hopes are laid.
Step forward, seek the heart's own way,
For the narrow path invites you to stay.

The Melancholy of Evening's Breath

As dusk descends, a gentle sigh,
The world adorned in twilight's dye.
Soft whispers dance in the cooling air,
A melody woven with tender care.

The horizon blushes, kissed by night,
Stars awaken, blinking their light.
Yet in the beauty, a tremble resides,
A lingering shadow, where hope divides.

Crickets strum their mournful song,
Echoes of memories, both weak and strong.
In the stillness, hearts may ache,
For dreams deferred and bonds that break.

Moonbeams cast on paths untread,
Illuminating stories left unsaid.
Each breath of evening, a soft lament,
Whispers of love, forever spent.

But in the sorrow, a grace unfolds,
For the night wraps secrets like stories told.
In evening's breath, we find what's true,
The melancholy whispers, guiding us through.

Fates Woven in the Winds Beneath

In the tapestry of stars, fates entwine,
Threads of chance in patterns divine.
With each breeze, a whisper is found,
Stories carried from the lost ground.

Beneath the sky's vast, watchful eye,
Promises flit like birds in flight.
Each moment, a stitch in destiny's seam,
Woven with wishes and unspoken dreams.

The winds speak softly to those who will hear,
Echoing tales of joy and fear.
In every breath, a choice to make,
The road unfolds with every step we take.

Fates like threads in a delicate loom,
Interlace moments, dispel the gloom.
And with each gust, the world may sway,
Guided by winds that lead our way.

So follow the whispers, trust where they lead,
For in the chaos, we find what we need.
Fates woven gently in the winds beneath,
A dance of life in joyous bequeath.

The Reflective Surface of Solitude

In silence deep, I find my place,
A mirror's gaze, a quiet space.
Reflections dance in shadows cast,
Whispers of moments, both slow and fast.

Time stretches thin, like gossamer thread,
Carrying memories, both sweet and dread.
In solitude's arms, I learn to see,
The hidden layers that shape me free.

Each thought a ripple on the still pond,
Revealing the heart's true respond.
In this haven, where fears reside,
I confront the echoes that I must guide.

Amidst the quiet, truths take flight,
Finding solace in the depths of night.
The reflective surface, a canvas bare,
Invites the soul to lay itself there.

Through solitude's lens, clarity blooms,
In the calm, the spirit assumes.
To dance with shadows, to breathe the light,
Is to embrace the art of the night.

Faded Wings Beneath the Ashen Sky

In twilight's grasp, the shadows sigh,
Faded wings, where dreams once fly.
Beneath the ash, the stories lie,
Whispers lost, but never die.

The moon, a ghost, doth softly weep,
For fragile hearts that dare to leap.
In silence wrapped, our secrets keep,
As night unfolds, and stars do creep.

Through brambles thick, we wend our way,
With fading light, we cannot stay.
Yet hope ignites the darkest day,
In every heart, a place to sway.

Upon the breeze, a song so clear,
Of distant realms we hold so dear.
While ashes fall and dreams appear,
We chase the night, devoid of fear.

And in the dark, our spirits sing,
For every loss, a new beginning.
From faded wings, a tale we bring,
As dawn approaches, hearts take wing.

Glimmers of Silver in the Gloom

In shadows deep, where secrets weave,
Glimmers of silver we perceive.
A dance of light, so hard to believe,
In every heart, a tale we grieve.

Through misty veils, the stars do weep,
Echoes of dreams we wished to keep.
As moments fade, our hopes run steep,
Yet lingering there, the memories leap.

With fleeting breath, we wander far,
In search of light, our guiding star.
Though darkness falls, we bear the scar,
In every heart, we find the spar.

And when the dawn begins to wake,
The silver glints, our fears forsake.
In every breath, a path we take,
For every loss, a new heartache.

With every step, we chase the light,
Through endless night, our spirits fight.
For in the gloom, we find delight,
In glimmers soft, our souls ignite.

The Restless Eyes of the Night

The restless eyes of night awake,
In shadows where the silence breaks.
With whispered winds and dreams to make,
We wander paths, our fears to shake.

Beneath the stars, our secrets lie,
In every breath, a silent cry.
For moonlight casts a gentle sigh,
While restless hearts begin to fly.

Through haunted woods, the echoes call,
Each step we take, we fear the fall.
Yet in the dark, we claim it all,
For every rise, we dare the crawl.

With shadows dancing in the haze,
We find our way through winding ways.
The restless eyes, a fiery blaze,
In every loss, a new embrace.

As dawn approaches, night takes flight,
Yet still we seek, with all our might.
For in the dark, we find the light,
In restless dreams, our spirits write.

Echoes of Ancient Guardians

In whispers soft, the ancients speak,
Echoes of guardians, brave and meek.
Through time's embrace, their spirits peek,
In every heart, their wisdom seek.

With stories etched in stone and air,
The weight of worlds, a timeless care.
In every glance, their souls lay bare,
As shimmering light begins to share.

Through twilight's veil, their presence stirs,
In rustling leaves, their memory purrs.
Though ages pass, their legacy blurs,
In every heart, their light demurs.

With every step on hallowed ground,
Ancient paths where dreams are found.
The echoes ring, their truths unbound,
In every breath, their songs resound.

As starlit skies bear witness true,
The guardians whisper, old yet new.
In every soul, their spirit grew,
For in our hearts, their love shines through.

Secrets of the Winged Guardians

In shadows deep, they softly glide,
With whispered wings, they fear not the tide.
Guardians of realms, yet unseen by most,
In windswept heights, they watch and they boast.

Ancient tales in their eyes do twinkle,
Of magic woven and charms that sprinkle.
They carry dreams through the starry night,
With silent grace, they take to flight.

Lost in the dance of each fleeting breeze,
They echo secrets spoke under trees.
A symphony sung in the quietest hour,
Revealing the world's hidden power.

In moonlit glades, where the shadows play,
They guard the hopes of the night and day.
With each gentle flap, the stories unfold,
Of fierce loyalty and treasures untold.

So listen close, as the night unfurls,
For the guardians weave magic in swirls.
Their secrets, they keep, a wondrous refrain,
In the heart of the night, forever remain.

Celestial Lanterns in Gloom

Amidst the dark, where shadows creep,
The lanterns glow, secrets to keep.
Like stars reborn from forgotten night,
They flicker softly, casting their light.

Each ember holds a story profound,
Of whispered dreams that gather 'round.
In every flicker, a wish takes flight,
Guiding lost souls through endless night.

In silence, they flicker, still and bright,
Creating paths from shadows to light.
With hope anew, they softly gleam,
Awakening hearts to dare and dream.

They dance with the wind, a gentle sway,
A tender touch to night's dark play.
For in their glow, the world transforms,
As destiny bends and the heart conforms.

So hold your dreams close, the lanterns guide,
Through tangled fears, let love abide.
In every corner where darkness looms,
Shine bright, dear souls, like celestial blooms.

The Thrum of Forgotten Legends

In ancient woods where echoes reside,
The thrum of legends begins to abide.
A heartbeat found in the rustling leaves,
Whispers of heroes who dared to believe.

Time weaves its magic through stories long past,
In every gust of wind, those moments are cast.
With every step, the ground softly hums,
The tales of yore where adventure comes.

Beneath the full moon, shadows entwine,
Capturing dreams in their midnight design.
A tapestry rich with valor and grace,
Written in starlight, time can't erase.

Through valleys of mist and over the hills,
The echoes of laughter and perilous thrills.
They dance in the twilight, remember the fight,
As the thrum of legends ignites the night.

So heed the call of the stories untold,
For within their embrace, the brave hearts unfold.
In whispers of ages, find courage anew,
For the thrum of forgotten legends is true.

Where Horizon Meets the Echoed Memories

Where the horizon brushes the sky's soft hues,
Echoes of memories whisper their views.
Each sunset carries a tale untold,
Of moments lost, yet forever bold.

With golden rays that paint the sea,
The past awakens, yearning to be free.
As twilight descends, the shadows play,
Recalling dreams from the light of day.

On the breeze, a soft sigh, like a lover's song,
Stirring the heart where it once belonged.
In the lull of dusk, nostalgia blooms,
A wistful reminder of joy and its glooms.

Memories linger where the earth meets the sky,
In every soft ripple, in every sigh.
With colors entwining, they beckon the soul,
To cherish the past and let it unfold.

So treasure the moments, let echoes remain,
For where horizon meets memory's chain.
In the depths of twilight, our spirits ascend,
Embracing the echoes, we find our true blend.

A Symphony Beneath the Gloaming

In twilight's embrace, the stars align,
Whispers of magic, a gentle design.
The wind carries tales from yonder shore,
As night wraps the world in its silken lore.

Moonbeams dance lightly on the rippling stream,
While shadows entwine in a silvery dream.
Each note of the night sings secrets so deep,
Awakening spirits from slumber and sleep.

The trees sway to rhythms, a hushed serenade,
As echoes of laughter through shadows parade.
With every soft sigh, the evening replies,
A symphony woven with nature's soft sighs.

Crickets and owls join in the refrain,
Their voices like threads in a rich, vibrant chain.
Nature's own orchestra, vibrant and clear,
Plays not just for us, but for all who draw near.

As the gloaming descends, we're wrapped in its grace,
Lost in its beauty, in this sacred space.
Each melody lingers, a spell we can't break,
While dreams take to flight in the stillness we make.

Eyes of the Enigmatic Sky

Beneath the vast cloak of twilight's embrace,
The heavens unfold with a mystical grace.
Stars like reflections of secrets untold,
Invite us to wander where mysteries bold.

A canvas of wonders, azure and deep,
In whispers of twilight, the cosmos will speak.
Each shimmer a promise that beckons us near,
With eyes of the enigmatic sky so clear.

Clouds drift like dreams, in a silken ballet,
While constellations twinkle and softly play.
A galaxy's heart beats a rhythm divine,
And we trace the paths where the stardust aligns.

In moments of silence, we hear their refrain,
Echoes of longing that dance in our veins.
As evening embraces, with a hush we comply,
Gazing in wonder at the infinite sky.

With each fleeting thought, like a comet's bright tail,
We sail through the night, where dreams never fail.
For in every glance through this cosmic design,
Lies the essence of magic, both endless and fine.

Veils of Time Enshrouded in Mist

In the realm where the past meets the whispering air,
Veils of time linger, a tapestry rare.
Mists swirl around secrets from ages long past,
Capturing echoes that forever will last.

A river of moments flows softly yet deep,
In the arms of the fog, both enchanting and steep.
Memories linger like shadows at dusk,
Holding the whispers of love, loss, and trust.

Pathways entwined where the heartbeats reside,
Through the shrouded embrace, we wander, confide.
Each breath a reminder of what came before,
As the mist wraps around us, a soft, tender door.

We delve into twilight, where memories gleam,
In the depth of the fog, we awaken the dream.
Each moment a treasure, each sigh a soft kiss,
In the veils of time wrapped in mystical bliss.

So let us step gently into shadows that sway,
Where the past and the present emerge in the gray.
For in every soft shroud of the mist that we roam,
Lies the heart of our history, our timeless home.

Echoes from the Crest of Solitude

High on the crest where silence resides,
Whispers of time float on soft, gentle tides.
The world fades away in this haven of peace,
Where echoes of solitude grant sweet release.

A place for the heart to untangle its threads,
Where sorrows are lifted, and hope gently spreads.
In the quiet embrace of the mountain's steep height,
We find in our stillness the strength to ignite.

Each breath is a promise, each moment a gift,
As we tread lightly where shadows may drift.
With nature around us, our spirits entwined,
We forge a connection, both tender and kind.

In the symphony woven from whispers and sighs,
We gather the echoes that dance in the skies.
For in solitude's arms, the heart learns to sing,
And find in the quiet the joy that it brings.

So let echoes guide us, wherever we roam,
To the crest of our being, our timeless home.
In the silence, we rise, above worry and fear,
Finding solace in echoes of truth ever clear.

When Shadows Rise with Gilded Wings

In twilight's hush, the whispers call,
Soft secrets drift where shadows fall.
With gilded wings, they soar on high,
Embracing dreams as stars reply.

The moonlight weaves a silken thread,
Through ancient woods where spirits tread.
With every beat, the heart takes flight,
As shadows rise to greet the night.

Beneath the boughs of emerald shade,
The vibrant hues of dusk parade.
A dance of light, a fleeting glimpse,
Where magic stirs and silence winks.

In realms where fears begin to blend,
The twilight's song will never end.
With gilded wings, we take our stand,
And write our fate with trembling hands.

So linger here, let dreams unfold,
In shadowed tales of brave and bold.
For when shadows rise to take their flight,
We'll chase our hopes into the night.

Dreaming with the Winged Ancestors

In dreams, we dance on feathered flight,
Across the realms of starry light.
With winged ancestors by our side,
We journey forth, in grace and pride.

Their whispers guide us through the dark,
With secrets held in every spark.
Their laughter echoes in the breeze,
A melody that puts us at ease.

Through ancient woods, where shadows play,
Their stories lead us on our way.
With every beat of wings in flight,
They weave our dreams into the night.

We gather tales of long-lost days,
In whispered winds and twilight rays.
Their wisdom lingers, strong and true,
As we embrace the skies of blue.

So spread your wings and take the chance,
In dreams where spirits weave their dance.
For with the winged, we rise, we soar,
And find the magic evermore.

The Silent Sentinels of the Night

Beneath the cloak of midnight's grace,
The sentinels guard each sacred place.
With watchful eyes, they stand so still,
A testament of ancient will.

Across the field, the shadows creep,
As secrets hidden softly sleep.
In hushed reverence, they mark the hour,
Beneath the watch of starlit power.

With every rustle of the leaves,
Their silent watch the night receives.
A flicker here, a sigh of wind,
In every pause, their strength rescinds.

They guide the lost, they hold the tense,
And weave through dreams a soul's suspense.
Their quiet strength in darkness found,
A sacred bond that knows no bound.

So next you roam the night to find,
The silent sentinels behind.
For in their gaze, we find our way,
Through shadows deep till break of day.

An Elegy for the Feathered Whisperers

In twilight's hush, they weave their song,
Soft echoes lost, where hearts belong.
Pink-tipped wings in the evening glow,
Whispers of dreams, too fragile to show.

Winds carry tales from far-off lands,
Of unseen threads and gentle hands.
Through woven branches, their voices twine,
A fleeting moment, forever divine.

Yet shadows loom as day takes flight,
And silence falls, embracing night.
The sky bleeds colors, deep and bold,
Revealing stories yet to be told.

Oh feathered friends, on softest breeze,
Your songs remain, like rustling leaves.
In every flutter, a memory stays,
A soft lament, no words can phrase.

The Harmony of Lost Dreams

In corners dark, where wishes fade,
The quiet heart is gently weighed.
Once vibrant hopes, now whispers thin,
Entwine like threads of what has been.

Each sigh unfurls a tale of yore,
Of laughter bright, and spirits soar.
Yet shadows dance where daylight wanes,
And dreams drift softly, tethered chains.

A symphony of paths not trod,
Woven with fate, it feels so odd.
In silken strands, the echoes call,
In gentle nudges that rise and fall.

Yet deep in night, a spark ignites,
Hope finds its voice in hushed delights.
For even lost, they softly gleam,
A lullaby of a fleeting dream.

Glories of the Celestial Canopy

Beneath a dome of twinkling stars,
Our dreams awake, devoid of scars.
The moon, a lantern, guides the night,
In shimmering glances, pure delight.

Constellations weave a tale so bright,
Of ancient lore and endless flight.
In their glow, we seek and find,
The whispers held in cosmic mind.

A tapestry of hopes and fears,
Woven with laughter, threaded tears.
Galaxies dance, a wondrous sight,
Reminding us of the boundless light.

The heavens stretch in all their grace,
Holding mysteries we long to chase.
In visions vast, our spirits soar,
Guided by stars forever more.

Quivering Hues at Dusk's Door

As day takes breath and softly fades,
A palette spills where light invades.
Blush of pink and gold's embrace,
Marks the horizon with a gentle grace.

In whispers of twilight's tender kiss,
The world transforms, a painted bliss.
Every hue, a story told,
In vibrant shades, both warm and cold.

Shadows lengthen, night unfurls,
Mysteries shroud the hidden pearls.
Stars begin their delicate fall,
As dusk awakens, casting its call.

So linger here as day departs,
Each fading ray, an artist's heart.
For in this moment, beauty sings,
Quivering colors that twilight brings.

The Sorrow of Lost Aspirations

In the quiet hours of twilight's glow,
Dreams like whispers fade, soft and low.
Hearts once aflame, now heavy with chains,
Yearning for paths where hope gently wanes.

Beneath the starlit veil of regret,
Promises linger like shadows we met.
Each fleeting wish a star that fell,
Echoes of futures we dared not tell.

Chasing the echoes of glory's sweet song,
Voices of triumph, to whom do they belong?
Faded ambitions weave through the night,
Lost in the maze of forgotten light.

Time, a thief with an elegant hand,
Steals what we cherish, turns dreams to sand.
Yet in the ashes of sorrow's domain,
Flickers of hope rise, despite the pain.

So let the heart bear its weight with grace,
Each scar a reminder, time won't erase.
For in the dark, a glimmer persists,
A promise of dawn, in the clenching fists.

Flickers of Night in the Lamented Woods

Beneath the boughs where the shadows creep,
Whispers of night in the silence weep.
Flickers of hope in the dimming glade,
Stars intertwine with the dreams we've made.

The moon drapes silver on roots overgrown,
Secrets of ages that nature has sown.
Each sighing breeze tells a story of old,
Of lovers and legends, of treasures untold.

Glow-worms weave tales in the tapestry dark,
Their light is a flicker, a soft, gentle spark.
In the lamented woods where shadows dance,
Echoes of laughter invite a sweet chance.

Yet time moves softly, a blanket of dust,
Covering dreams in a blanket of rust.
But even in loss, the embers will glint,
For within us lies hope, a warm, steady hint.

So heed the call of the night's gentle breeze,
Where wishes take flight on the sighs of the trees.
In the lamented woods, find peace amid strife,
For in every flicker, there lies a new life.

Scrolls of Ages Between the Fates

In the shadowed tomes where silence holds sway,
Scrolls of ages whisper truths in decay.
Tales of the weary, of battles once fought,
Threads of our lives in the fabric of thought.

Fates intertwined in a dance with the stars,
Each parchment a journey through wounds and through
scars.
In ink of regret, in the margins of time,
Stories of heartache, of struggle, and rhyme.

Whispers of wisdom in each crinkled line,
A tapestry woven, rich with design.
The destinies shift, like the tides on the coast,
Yet in every chapter, it's hope we treasure most.

Across the ages, as seasons unfold,
Dreams written boldly, in stories retold.
Each scroll a reminder, of all that we chase,
In the depths of despair, we still find our place.

So gather the scrolls, turn their pages with care,
For within every loss, lies a flicker to share.
The stories are endless, like stars in the sky,
Scrolls of our fates in the blink of an eye.

Cinders of Memory in the Dimming Light

As shadows grow long in the fading day,
Cinders of memory begin to stray.
Flickering softly in twilight's embrace,
Fragments of laughter, love's tender trace.

The embers of moments once vividly bright,
Glint in the darkness, a glimmering sight.
Yet time drifts on, with its gentle embrace,
Turning bright flames into soft ash and space.

In the cradle of dusk, where dreams intertwine,
Memories linger, then gently decline.
But even the cinders can spark a new flame,
Whispering softly of love without name.

Through the night's quiet, their warmth we embrace,
Carrying stories and threads of our grace.
In the tapestry woven of light and of shade,
Every flicker of memory shall never fade.

So gather the cinders, let them take flight,
In the heart's gentle glow, find the lost light.
For even in darkness, hope finds its way,
In the cinders of memory, love's bright ballet.

www.ingramcontent.com/pod-product-compliance
Ingram Content Group UK Ltd.
Pitfield, Milton Keynes, MK11 3LW, UK
UKHW021318280125
4330UKWH00005B/312